PAM HALL

The Coil
a history
in four parts
1988-1993

curated by Patricia Grattan

catalogue essays by Patrick O'Flaherty
and Nancy Shaw

Art Gallery, Memorial University of Newfoundland
St. John's, Newfoundland, Canada
1994

ACKNOWLEDGMENTS

The artist gratefully acknowledges financial assistance from the Canada Council, and the Newfoundland and Labrador Arts Council.

The artist is deeply grateful for additional support from NICHIRO CORP. in Tokyo, whose assistance made possible the sitework in Kyushu, Japan.

Fishery Products International in St. John's, played a significant role in the Coil's journey to Japan, and the artist is grateful for their interest and support.

The artist is indebted to Patricia Grattan, Memorial University of Newfoundland, and to the staff of Open Space in Victoria and the New Gallery in Calgary, for facilitating the Canadian sitework and exhibiting its results.

Acknowledgment of those individuals who have made the entire process possible through their personal assistance and support is detailed on page 51.

The publication of this catalogue was assisted by support from the Canada/Newfoundland Agreement on Cultural Industries.

Published in conjunction with the exhibition <u>The Coil: a history in four parts</u> organized by Memorial University Art Gallery, St. John's, Newfoundland, and presented at the Art Gallery of the Canadian Embassy in Tokyo, Japan in January, 1994, and at Canadian galleries in 1994-1995.

Tour Itinerary:

Art Gallery of the Canadian Embassy, Tokyo, Japan
Memorial University Art Gallery, St. John's, Newfoundland
Confederation Centre for the Arts, Charlottetown, P.E.I.
Art Gallery of Southern Alberta, Lethbridge, Alberta
Art Gallery of Thunder Bay, Thunder Bay, Ontario

Catalogue co-published by Pam Hall and Memorial University Art Gallery

Designed by: Pam Hall

Printed by Dicks and Company, St. John's

Film by fotoGRAFIX, St. John's

Reproduction Photography of the Biographical Notes: Ned Pratt

All other photography: Pam Hall

ISBN 0-88901-256-3

Memorial
University of Newfoundland

Contents

The Coil *on site... (clockwise from top left)*

Middle Cove Beach, Newfoundland, 1988

Futamigaura, Kyushu, Japan, 1993

near Milk River, Alberta, 1991

Harling Point, Victoria, B.C., 1990

The Coil that Binds, the Line that Bends...
an introduction

The Coil That Binds, the Line That Bends is a process of site-responsive environmental installation and subsequent studio work that has engaged Pam Hall for the past five years. Memorial University's Art Gallery gave the early Newfoundland Coil works their first public exposure in our 1989 exhibition, MASKUNOW A Trail A Path. We now are presenting selected works representing the entire project in **The Coil - a History in Four Parts**, an exhibition that we are pleased to be sharing with a Japanese audience and with other Canadian galleries.

Those who know Pam Hall know she has a way with words as well as with images. And it seems to me that Hall as author is very much in evidence in the Coil works — not only in the poetic incantatory phrases and the Biographical Notes, which are like pages from a journal, but in the basic structure of the project.

The Coil is the protagonist in a narrative the artist is "writing". It (or she as Hall refers to the Coil) comes into the story with a pre-history made of its physical origin, as a cod trap, and its symbolic associations for Hall. These, which have been reflected in most of the artist's earlier bodies of work, include cycles of birth and death, fecundity, ritual, the relationship of humans and nature. The narrative proceeds as the artist works with the Coil at various outdoor locations across Canada and in Japan: the Coil acquires its own history, with each site providing both the setting and the source for a direct encounter with the physical world and, at the same time, forming "chapters" in an unfolding biography. It is a history of incidents, accidents, relationships and accretions from the sites and cultures in which it temporarily rests: Shinto religious practices, ancient rock formations in the Alberta badlands, tools of the fishing trade, clear cut evidence of exploitation of nature...

Working with images gathered on site and with her own intuitive response to remembered experience of the physical and human contexts of each encounter, Hall makes that history manifest in the Biographical Notes. Their shifting format and overlayered maps, drawing, images and texts reflect the nature of history — fragments of experience, tentative observations, enticing paths of inquiry. Helping us to trace our way through Hall's dense web of information and allusion are guest essayists Patrick O'Flaherty, St. John's and Nancy Shaw, Vancouver, whom we thank for their perceptions. We also want to acknowledge, for their essential assistance with the exhibition and catalogue, the cultural staff at The Canadian Embassy, Tokyo; The Canada Council, which remains a vital source of support for the arts in Canada; and Pam Hall, who has been an energetic and enthusiastic collaborator.

Patricia Grattan

The first circle... Middle Cove Beach, Newfoundland, 1988

Pam Hall and the Coil

Patrick O'Flaererty

Pam Hall has internalized the Newfoundland experience in a new way. To me, she resembles Rockwell Kent or even the writer Norman Duncan, both outsiders for whom Newfoundland became a spiritual home, both forced to experiment with artistic forms, to wrench them out of their traditional shapes, in order to express a shocked awareness of ocean and landscape.

Pam Hall too has had to look beyond the resources of conventional artistry to express what is stirred up in her,as woman and as a creator, by the elemental forces on this hard edge of the North American continent. Do not picture her as sitting on a headland with palette and brushes. Think of her rather as akin to T.S. Eliot: a poet of shards and scissors. Not for her the straight lines and numinousness of the magic realists. (There are neat lines on the edges of her works: but the twisting, turning, breaking forms within the boundaries seem a flight from what is shapely and fixed.)

No boats sit peacefully at anchor in her work. Throw words like idyll and rustic out of the skiff. She is in the business of inventing rather than inheriting forms; that's the only way she can tell what she has witnessed and felt. Her work does not just provide an image of life; it seems to participate in it in some way. Though purposeful underneath, it has in it the jaggedness of seascape, a littoral clutter, suggesting the untamed and shapeless forces of nature.

It is typical of her that her art springs from muscular contact with earth and ocean. The pleasures of the gazebo, sitting back and watching butterflies in the flowery meadow, are not her pleasures. She has gone out to confront and explore her world in a brazen fashion. She fishes, works, hauls, lifts rocks. Then creates out of the lifting and hauling. The hand that draws and takes photos has sores on it from the rub of real rope and the bones of real fish.

The Coil, *on the deck of the Whispering Sea ready to come ashore at Quidi Vidi, Newfoundland, 1988*

The first spiral... heavy with water on Elis wharf, Quidi Vidi, Newfoundland, 1988

She goes about her job of creation in a number of ways. She will make a scene with, say, driftwood, photograph it, photograph it again slightly altered, create a sequence of photographs, find a topographic map to place it over or under, alter the map with various devices of art - - then write about it, this mixture, as if meaning were too precious a commodity to be left entirely to the visible objects.

Or she will do it differently.

Throughout, as a dominant motif, there is the Coil.

A cod trap is an unwieldy, heavy object which demands the greatest care and skill of the fisherman or - woman if it is to catch fish. Knitting a trap is hard enough. Placing it in a skiff so it can be put out properly with a lop on is taxing too. But setting it in the salt water is the thing. Tides, depth of water, the shape of the bottom — all this and more must be understood; the leader, anchors, kegs, trap-mouth, all have to positioned just so. Get something a foot or so wrong, no fish. A successful trap-setter (as Hall well knows) is thus a kind of artist.

Hall's Coil — made by sewing part of a real, though discarded cod trap into a 110-foot length with red fishing twine — is not just the metaphor through which she replicates what she sees in the world of work and anxiety she has entered. It is her way of sharing the daily grind of the fishing life: the trap-man or -woman pulls the twine out of the water; Hall pulls the Coil (a "she", of course) into varying shapes. This ropy object is at different times, depending on how her hand shapes it — and what you, the viewer, are open to seeing in it — a nest, a string of kelp, a worm or snake or dragon, a long tail, a set of layers, the tentacles of some sea creature, a circle, a ring of circles, a puzzle, a contour line on a map, a whip, an umbilical cord, something dead, something living.

Every knot, as she says, a thought.

Sea-water wet and too heavy to lift by hand,
The Coil *being lowered by the winch onto Eli's wharf, Quidi Vidi, Newfoundland, 1988*

A trap is hard to handle, massive, heavy. So is the Coil, for it must be lugged around the world in a great bag to find a place to yield its significance. A beach, maybe. A hillside. A grassy field. The Alberta Badlands. Japan, even. The floor of a gallery. But always it summons up the sea and the things that lurk in it and the life of the men and women who toil on it and near it.

Coil means spiral, vortex, gyre, spring. It is something wound up, a force contained, one that can be unleashed. There is energy pent up in Hall's work. An impression of energy and motion is the first thing we get from her work. There is a daring in it too, a willingness to toy with broken images, to make art out of flotsam. And there is a woman's wish — no, not wish merely, a fierce determination — to see this strange, grim world in a woman's way, truly, not being restricted to the traditional linear modes defined by men and showing how men think.

Hall is off on a sea-voyage of her own. We can follow in her wake. If she seems, at first, to lead us into unfamiliar waters, be advised she is steering by her own compass and stars. Following, we soon become more at ease, for she is an artist. The ship is in good hands.

What does art do? To answer this question, Wallace Stevens used the metaphor of a jar:

> *I placed a jar in Tennessee,*
> *And round it was, upon a hill.*
> *It made the slovenly wilderness*
> *Surround that hill.*
>
> *The wilderness rose up to it,*
> *And sprawled around, no longer wild.*
> *The jar was round upon the ground*
> *And tall and of a port in air.*

Though both are "round upon the ground", I prefer Pam Hall's Newfoundland Coil to Stevens' Tennessee jar. The jar, Stevens insists, has "dominion" over the wilderness; it organizes and subdues it. But Hall's Coil, unlike the jar, is a part of the world of flux and motion. It lies next to the wilderness too but, though it seeks and makes connections, leaves it slovenly and primitive. It is art that coexists with what is wild and true.

*Three lines on the land... **The Coil** (from top to bottom) at Harling Point, Vancouver Island, 1990, in the Drumheller Badlands, and near East Coulee, Alberta 1991*

A Time Between Times

Nancy Shaw

> Ritual takes place in the temporal framework of myth,
> in that Celtic "time between times" of twilights, mist,
> and hybrids which John Sharkey has compared to the
> "entrelacs" of Celtic visual arts, the visual knots
> and puns and curves– repetitive images arising from
> tasks set the contemplative mind.
>
> –Lucy R. Lippard

Resistance to Western modes of domination– especially our alienated and divisive relationship to nature is charted by Pam Hall's five year expedition, **The Coil That Binds, the Line that Bends**. Suspended in the liminal space of ritual, she addresses the sense of loss perpetuated by patriarchal capitalism in site-specific landscape installations with **The Coil**– the floor of a cod trap reclaimed and intricately bound. Her journey of discovery draws connections between human labour and the land to form an intricate web of meaning akin to the life cycle of birth, growth, sacrifice and rebirth. This is all documented in the **Biographical Notes**, collages full of poetic and photographic elements. Layers of correspondence rife with symbolic resonance between past, present and future remind us of marginalized narratives, particular myths of ancient matriarchal societies celebrating the earth's association with the feminine. This is not an epic of heroic conquest. Hall's is a tale of regeneration and reflection arrived at through drawing, knotting, spiralling and binding.

Drawing - the long line

As with all stories of discovery, **The Coil's** begins with introductions, drawing interrelations between the tale's various elements – setting a scene against which the action can take place. Initiated by its birth, **The Coil** emerges as an artist's tool from a hunter's implement; **The Coil**; Hall says "falls artlessly onto the land" and its making has quite a history. While a set director on a film shoot, Hall become engrossed in one location, Quidi Vidi Gut– a harbour in St. John's where she later learned to fish with Eli Tucker and sons. Fascinated by the process and history of this local inshore industry, she launched her Coil, mimicking fishing gestures and imbuing her artistic practice with a ritual social function.

Through an arduous and labour-intensive process, with red twine she hand-bound the floor of Eli's old cod trap into a 32m rope. After thirty-three days of preparation, **The Coil**, as she christened it, was ritually retrieved from the ocean's depths onto the long liner **Whispering Sea**. To celebrate its rebirth and acknowledge its history, Hall wrapped **The Coil** around the **Whispering Sea's** hold and placed it on the wharf in the shape of a nest.

The nest, like the net, is a space where one form of life sustains another to establish The Coil as both womb and tomb and create a dynamic tension upon which Hall's work thrives. Her appropriation of fishing gestures forges archetypal connection between the art of retrieving hidden meaning from unconscious depths and the laboured gathering of sustenance from the deep sea. Other rites she practised included the cleaning of salt water from The Coil and laying it on the land to dry. During certain times of the season it is not unusual in Newfoundland to see the land decorated with nets being cleaned and repaired.

In the face of drastic economic fluctuations, the inshore fishery still embodies vestiges of its pre-industrial form that coexisted symbolically with nature. Hall's artistic statement is instructive on the issue. She writes;

> **The Coil** emerged both physically and conceptually from one of the last remaining **primitive** interactions between humans and Nature ...the fishery of inshore Newfoundland. Primitive in that it is direct, unmeditated, and full of both terror and comfort... primitive in that it is a vestige of the hunt...one of the first and formative ways the species interacted in the natural world...and primitive in that the distance between hunter and the hunted is minimal, the technology used is ancient and simple, and the relationship with the natural world is still bound by respect and dependency, rather than by mastery and control.

The Coil, wrapping the hold of the Whispering Sea, North Atlantic, 1988

The Coil's reincarnation establishes it as an object with a tangible history while its future resides in the potential of a more integrated relationship with nature. Nevertheless, **The Coil** takes into account the current strife of inshore fisheries. After years of immense offshore depletions and federal mismanagement, a moratorium has been placed on the cod fishery; this moratorium undermines the age-old cultural and economic fabric of Newfoundland. In the tradition of a long line of cultural nationalists, Pam Hall's work doubles as an allegory of lament and resistance to federal and multinational colonization by asserting the origins and elements of local culture.

In Newfoundland, **The Coil's** siting traces elements that contributed to an integrated relationship with nature in a pre-industrial fishing economy. At Middle Cove Beach and Hawke Hill Barrens, **The Coil's** circle and spiral configurations explore the dynamics of culture rooted in the balance between domestic husbandry and hunting. The beach-work traverses the personal and domestic – incidentally Middle Cove is visited by many local families including Hall's own during the summer. Circling small stones, **The Coil** celebrates their symbolic association with fertility, femininity and ancient matriarchal rites. These configurations also refer to Hall's earlier work such as the watercolours of the same rocks (**Stone Circles, 1984**) and the **Callanish Diaries** (1986), drawings derived from experiences of the ancient rock formations in Scotland. At Hawke Hill Barrens, the tensions of the life cycle become more pronounced. **The Coil** placed as a serpent (the symbol for fertility) at the foot of a hunter's rock commemorates the hunter's bounty once gathered on what is now craggy, barren land, eroded by weather and time.

Nesting near the Hunter's Stone, Hawke Hill Barrens, Newfoundland, 1988

Knotting - for each knot, a thought

While there is much to be learned from **The Coil** configurations in Newfoundland, every good tale gains momentum with the introduction of obstacles - prompting all involved to learn from the unexpected contradictions set out before them. Many disconcerting configurations emerged around **The Coil** during her journey to Vancouver island.

Although Hall did not consciously intend to replicate **The Coil's** formations at home, echoes emerged and illuminated the links between the two locales. Both are islands, relatively isolated from the mainland with dependent resource-based economies set in a tremendous and variant landscape.

In addition to these initial bonds, **The Coil's** settings mirror in many ways those in Newfoundland. This, of course, is reflected in the direction of her travel – from east to west, from sunrise to sunset – inhabiting polar extents of the daily cycle. Initially Hall planned that Eli's wharf at Quidi Vidi would be its only human-made setting. However, in British Columbia, this aim proved impossible. On Vancouver Island she discovered that many non-urban settings were indelibly marked by human exploitation. Hall, disturbed by this treatment of the land, later emphasized the conflictual relations between culture and nature in the **Biographical Notes**, unlike in those from Newfoundland where she celebrated the organic interdependence of the two.

One example of equivalent settings was when **The Coil** was set up in a clear cut near the Jordan Ridge on land made barren by the expedient but ruthless logging practices rather than the forces of time and weather that contribute to the state of Hawke Hill Barrens. After visiting this clear cut, Hall likened **The Coil** to a line running through this ruin infusing it with life in much the same way as the holy river Jordan is one of the only freshwater sources in the Middle East. The Jordan River is, of course, a line of life as well as a object of great political strife. On a personal note, Hall's daughter' name is Jordan leading her to deem this site "her daughter's land laid waste." She visited recreational beaches – French Beach and one at East Sooke. Impressed by the large driftwood trunks, she nestled **The Coil** in and amongst this wood washed smooth and preserved by the sea. She made circles (reminiscent of Middle Cove) and winding lines reminding her of her IUD – a reproductive barrier signifying human intervention in the life cycle. The long and elastic curves traced in the East Sooke sand formed stretch marks – lines of the productive transformations of life etched impermanently in the delicate skin of the body and the beach.

In the city, the dissonant relationship between culture and nature became more glaring. During impromptu set-ups done in and around the Chinese Cemetery at Harling Point in Victoria, **The Coil** nested on the graveyard's principal monument, a memorial to the Chinese railway workers exploited by the forces of industrial development and nationalism. On the rocks below the cemetery bound by the Pacific Ocean, **The Coil** traced glacial scars. Much to the surprise of the artist, the composition formed a uterine shape later tangled with washed-up debris – freshly used condoms and a medical syringe – forming a paradoxical emblem of her experience on the West Coast. **The Coil**, here as in the other landscapes, traced the fine line between life and death, exploitation and sustenance, nature and culture.

Uterine on the rocks at Harling Point,
Vancouver Island, 1990

Although it was not her intention to explore divisive dichotomies between culture and nature when she started in Newfoundland, the course of her journey led her to these exploitive relations that permeate most aspects of the material world. For instance, the language of the **Biographical Notes** recalls the tension between the joyous beginning of **The Coil's** birth and to the knotting contradictions that emerged in B.C. In Newfoundland notes, rhythmic, intuitive incantations describe **The Coil's** beginnings:

> *out of the belly*
> *she came – alive*
> *out of the gut – steamed five –*
>
> *– and so it starts*
> *my berth*
> *its birth*
> *pulled aboard –umbilical cord*
> *tying me – we, the three*
> *binding – me, to she*
> *trapping the time*
> *hiding the line*
> *a drift on the salt-sweet sea*

The language of the B.C. notes, however, provides a sure contrast through weighty, clashing dissonance denoting a shift form automatic writing to more analytic language.
Note her comparison of fishing and logging terminologies:

wound - - rip	nest - - coiled
burn - - strip	forest - - spoiled
slash - - gut	burnt - - ground
clear - - cut	trap - - bound

Serpentine in the slash, near Jordan River,
Vancouver Island, 1990

Spiralling - the unclosed circle

While **The Coil** led her to explore the costs of human sacrifice and devastation of land by forces of industrial progress, her journey to the Alberta Badlands lent perspective to the contradictions previously established between the explosive relations of the present and the interdependent economics of the recent past. The Badlands journey constituted a spiral movement back in time, returning to the source of a distant geological past. Unlike linear returns that consider the past a dead object and rarely account for resonance and correspondence, the spiral is a continuum whose end points are equally integral and dynamic in the life cycle.

The Badlands, now a desert, was an inland sea roughly seventy-five million years ago. This wondrous terrain is maintained in a series of nature preserves such as Dinosaur Provincial Park and Writing on Stone Provincial Park. On a land barren of life and rich in history, Hall traces the past written on the landscape in her ritual process of "knowing through doing" Like other artists such as Michelle Stuart, Hall travels to ancient sites to enact contemporary versions of age-old rites respecting natural forces. Her work is temporary, small scale and ecological unlike most artists' earthworks that leave large and imposing marks on the land.

Pam Hall makes many plays on **The Coil's** red colour in order to further forge a symbolic continuum through time and space, **The Coil's** red line echoes the recording marks of ancient cultures: red ochre was used to draw pictographs in the Badlands. Red ochre was also used ritually by the Beothucks, (the aboriginal inhabitants encountered by the first white settlers in Newfoundland) to colour their skin and bury their dead. Due to colonial exploitation, the last of the Beothucks died in the nineteenth century. This is in part a gesture of remembrance similar to the Chinese graveyard memorial. Moreover, through the colour red, many connections are made with fishing culture in Newfoundland: for instance, buildings were once painted with a mixture of red ochre and fish oil. Fish spawning trenches are called reds. It is also a reference to the esteemed Newfoundland artist Don Wright (who recently passed away). Wright's sculpture **Red Trench**, commissioned for the St. John's Confederation Building, was censored because some were offended by their associations of the work with female genitalia. Hall's play on red imbues **The Coil** with resonances of fertility, communications, nourishment and cleansing of the body. This red line wraps itself around rocks, mounds and hoodoos, is run through dry river beds and along valley walls and drawn across the banks of the Red Deer River, becoming a membrane through which both productive and destructive energies pass.

In this dynamic spiralling continuum, The Coil spans time and space, life and death. The ephemeral present is impressed on the ancient past to situate contemporary manipulations of and coexistences with nature in a larger universal cycle. As such, the present emerges as one frame among others in this spiral of measurement, review, assessment and growth.

The Coil... two spirals on Vancouver Island, British Columbia, 1990 (top), and two in the Alberta Badlands, 1991 (bottom)

al, the Canadian Embassy, Tokyo, 1993

After situating Western conceptions of nature within a larger geological frame, Hall returns to the present to a multitude of personal, artistic, cultural and symbolic correspondences. An intricate web of meaning emerges, fleshing out her hopes of developing a harmonious existence with nature. To do this, she travelled to Japan, where unexpected connections emerged, allowing Hall to feel at home in unfamiliar surroundings. Remembering Newfoundland, she set up **The Coil** on beaches, fishing wharfs, as well as in gardens and at sacred shrines. She noted many similarities: Newfoundland and Japan are islands with thriving coastal cultures reliant on fishing to a certain extent, and are roughly the same geographical size. Both are identified as Eastern (although not in relationship to each other) and have been subject to colonial exploits. Nevertheless, records state that Japanese settlement is much older and more densely populated than Newfoundland (the population of Japan is 111,057,485 compared to Newfoundland's population of 567,681).

Japanese notions of nature were most striking to Hall, especially those that emerged through Shinto. Unlike Western Christianity, Shinto's spirits exist in the material world rather than outside and above it. In Shinto, there is no word for nature that situates humans as separate and dominant. Howard Fox states that in Shinto:

> ...man is equivalent to and involved with nature and the spirits and life force embodied therein, that the art object is the locus of the individual's spiritual encounter with nature, that the artist works "with" the materials to discover their "inner being," rather than against them to impose his technical virtuosity... [2]

Moreover, in both art and nature, arrangement and order are important as each component is integral to universal harmony. Even though nature in both Western Christianity and Shinto contexts is replete with human manipulations, the Japanese approach is based on order and harmony rather than domination, accumulation and consumption.

Near the Canadian Embassy in Tokyo, Hall circled **The Coil** around a pristine and highly arranged garden, most unlike the wind-worn and sea-sculpted terrain traced in Victoria's cityscape. Recalling the sittings on Eli's wharf, she set up **The Coil** at wharfs on the Japanese island of Kyushu, comparing fishing methods and tools to Newfoundland's. More transcultural comparisons emerge in the **Biographical Notes** where compositions resembled holy crosses, kimonos, and fishing oil-skins hung to dry.

Shimenawa, at a shrine in Hita, Kyushu, Japan, 1993

Hall visited spiritual places like Hita where she wrapped a Shinto shrine and traced a Sumo Ring. Significantly, rope is used for many sacred purposes in Japan, especially within Shinto, where each gateway to each shrine in draped with a shimenawa (sacred rope). Consequently, **The Coil** sitings were enriched by new contextual and symbolic meaning. Her trip to Futamigaura was perhaps the most revealing for Hall. She discovered Meoto-iwa – two rocks protruding from the sea bound by rope signifying their marriage. In this uncanny place she laid one significant rope leading to another. On a nearby beach she drew a circle marking the end of her journey... an echo of the first circle drawn on a Newfoundland beach five years earlier. She describes this as a signing off, a returning home in the process of running into her origins across the world. Perhaps the following poetic fragment best summarizes **The Coil's** acquired function in this work of discovery:

> *one rope tied*
> *by Shinto hands*
> *one laid down*
> *from distant land*
> *one for binding*
> *one for finding*
> *both bound by*
> *the sea – the sand*
> *one to lead*
> *a caring eye...*
> *one to wed*
> *two rocks to tie...*
> *one to map*
> *unveil a site...*
> *one to manifest*
> *a rite.*

Although in retrospect it is easy to recount the polyphony of symbolic resonance accumulating through out the five year project, it is crucial to note that the artist did not consciously plan the course of her journey. Her overriding concern resides in **The Coil's** physical encounter with and engagement in the landscape. The work and the process it emerges from , is ephemeral, non-intrusive, material-dependent and site-responsive. Moreover, **The Coil's** sitings are domestic in scale and greatly determined by such details as the weather and the crew she works with. As an engaged explorer, Hall is fully awake in the land, attentive and respectful, searching out methods of coexistence with nature.

1. Lucy R. Lippard, **Overlay** (New York: Pantheon, 1983) 160
2. Howard N. Fox, "A Primal Spirit", A Primal Spirit: Ten Contemporary Japanese Sculptors (Los Angeles County Museum of Art, 1991) 26

newfoundland
1988-1989

a line drawn
a drawn line
a bound trap
trap- bound
a berth on the water
a birth on the water
from a long-liner
comes a long line

one long line
from sea...to me

The Coil *on site in Newfoundland, 1988*
(from top to bottom)

Eli Tucker's wharf, Quidi Vidi

Hawke Hill barrens

Middle Cove Beach

Middle Cove Beach

first sign ~ first site
coiled line ~ in-sight

1

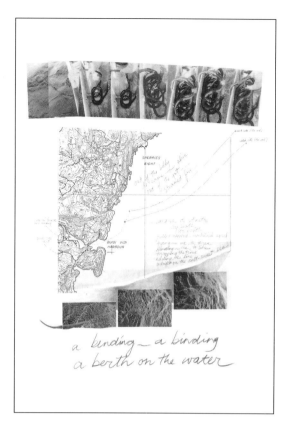

a binding — a binding
a berth on the water

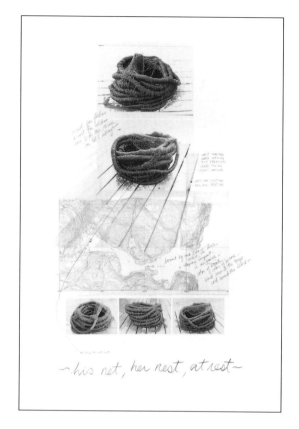

~his net, her nest, at rest~

2

out of the belly...
she came... alive
out of the gut...
steamed five

and so it starts,
my berth
its birth

pulled aboard
umbilical cord

tying... we, the three
binding... me, to She
trapping the time
holding the line,
adrift
on the salt-sweet sea

3

bound by red line
coiled, she lies...
a sleeping serpent
in disguise

color of blood
color of wine
bind round the trap
coil round the line

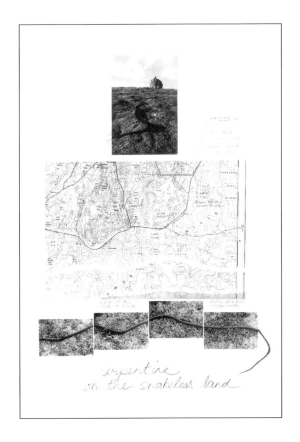

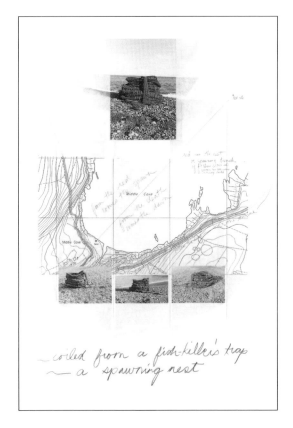

4

5

over land
she leads
barren-bound,
she lies

red to white
white to black

follow forward
follow back

red: noun
  a nest or spawning trench for fishes
(Webster's New 20th Century Dictionary,
2nd Edition.)

From the red
comes the spawn

from the death
comes the dawn

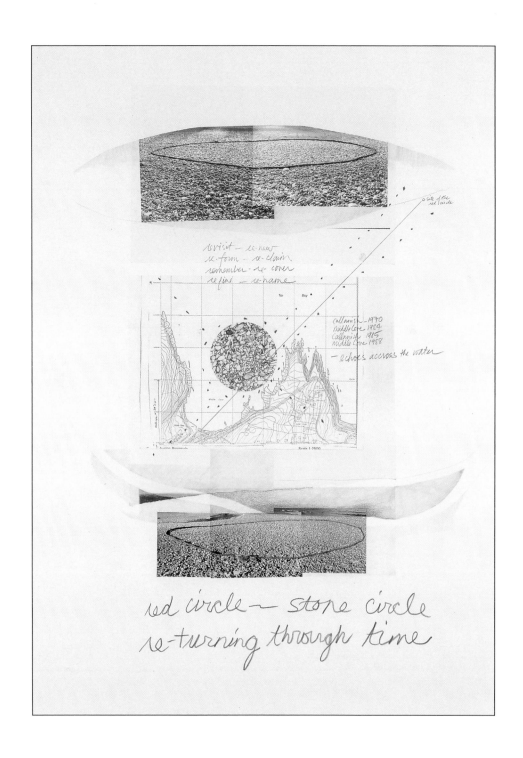

red circle — stone circle
re-turning through time

6

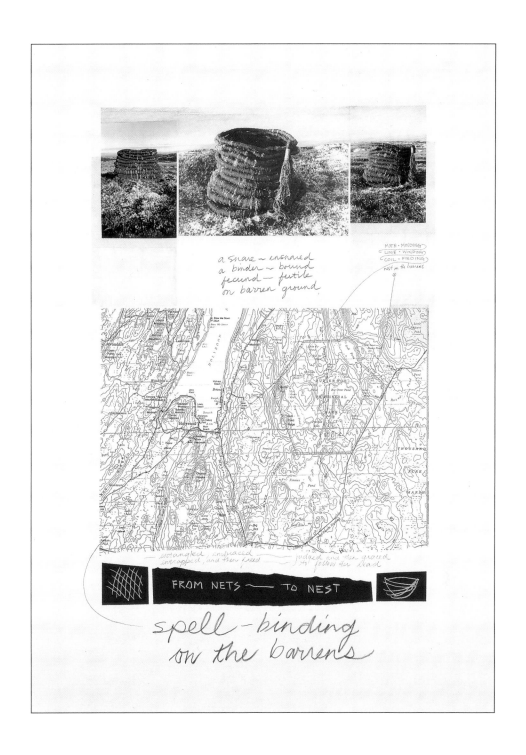

a snare ~ ensnared
a binder ~ bound
fecund ~ futile
on barren ground

MYTH · MINDING
LINE · WINDING
COIL · FINDING
nest on the barrens

entangled, embraced
enwrapped, and then freed

judged and fin graced
tis fellow fur dead

FROM NETS ⎯ TO NEST

spell-binding
on the barrens

7

List of Plates: *the Newfoundland Series*

1   first sign - first site... coiled line - in-sight

2   a bending, a binding... a berth on the water

3   his net, her nest, at rest

4   serpentine... in the snakeless land

5   coiled from a fish-killer's trap... a spawning nest

6   red circle - stone circle...re-turning through time

7   spell-binding...on the barrens

The works represented here were selected from a
series of 15 Newfoundland *Biographical Notes*.

vancouver island
1990

drawn - out to sea
drawn out - to see

The Coil on site on Vancouver Island, 1990
(from top to bottom)

Harling Point, Victoria

Ogden Point Seawall, Victoria

at French Beach

at East Sooke Beach

feng shui in the west

1

hugon - guarded in the west
re-turning east

concealed in the belly
revealed on the land

2

from one island to another
from one sea   to the other,
she turns, is drawn...... echoes

old mark	*new mark*
on stone	*on stone*
first sign	*same sign*
first site	*last site*
east sight	*west site*
on site	*in-sight*

3

insert	*exert*
imbed	*expel*
instill	*express*
infuse	*expose*

from inside out, she manifests
from belly to beach,
from east to west

overland she stretches
pulled to the sea

a coil on the beach
a coil in me

uprooted from the sacred grove
nesting in the west

4

a root... a source
a route... a course

to take root
to branch out
to stem from,
to stand

root......... over the land lies
a subterranean route

safe harboured
on the sea wall

5

from line to nest
from east to west

one shelter harbours another
one harbour shelters another

over grid... over ground
red line leading... harbour-bound

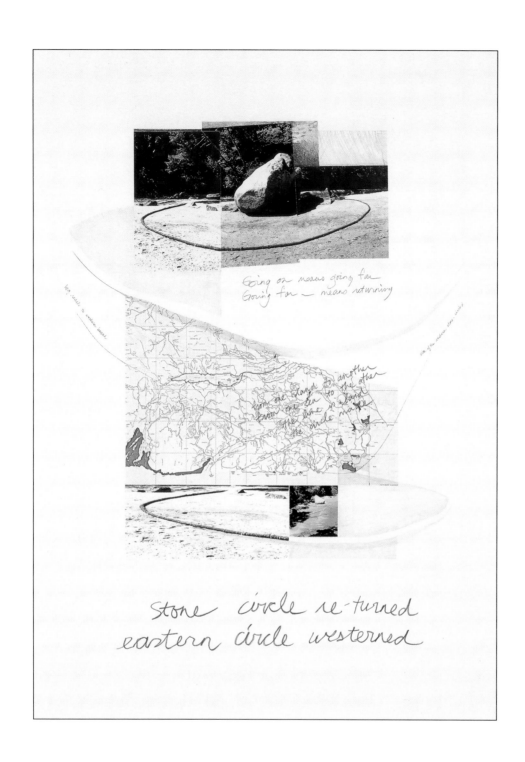

Going on means going far
Going far — means returning

stone circle re-turned
eastern circle westerned

6

On the last day there was only listening.
there were marks for following —
between the graveyard and the sea.

Death at her back
Saltwater at her face
she followed.

In a birth canal to the water
she lay — open-mouthed
between pelvic stones — bones.

the rest — wrenching line
found form to follow
stone and hollow
a womb — waiting to be drawn.

near her life side, sea side,
mouth — by the needle — empty
at her back below the graves
next morning by the safe. tall

artifacts — like her.
signs — in context
signs — of context

— uterine — she lies revealed
between the cradle and the grave

7

List of Plates: *the Vancouver Island Series*

1   feng shui in the west

2   dragon-guarded in the west...re-turning east

3   concealed in the belly... revealed on the land

4   uprooted...in the sacred grove

5   safe-harboured...on the sea wall

6   stone circled re-turned...eastern circle - westerned

7   uterine - she lies revealed...
       between the cradle and the grave

The works represented here were selected from
a series of 13 Biographical Notes from Vancouver Island .

alberta badlands
1991

sky in the water
clouds on the earth
old bones sing for death
red nest sings for birth

from river to sky
from water to sand
bound... by the river
freed...on the land

The Coil on site in the Alberta Badlands, 1991
(from top to bottom)

near East Coulee

Dinosaur Provincial Park

Writing on Stone Provincial Park

near Drumheller

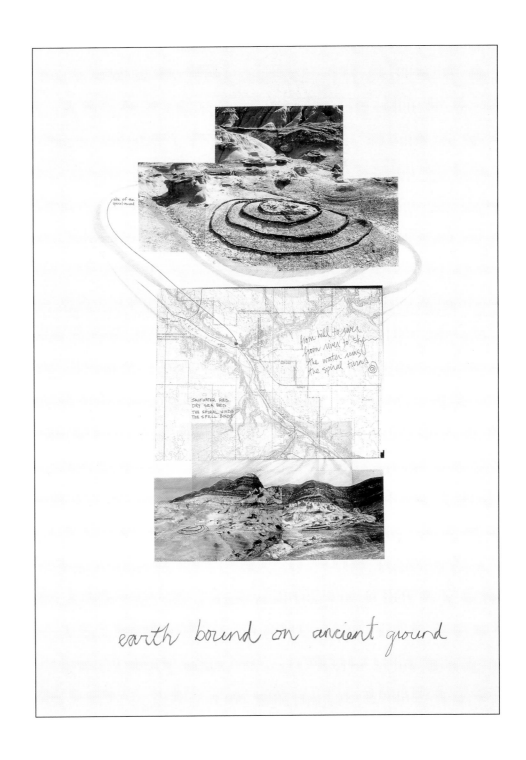

SALTWATER RED
DRY SEA BED
THE SPIRAL WINDS
THE SPELL BINDS

from hill to river
from river to sky
the water runs
the spiral turns

earth bound on ancient ground

1

coiled, red, in the river bed
cradled — in the grave

a transient line
writing on stone

2

earth - Altar   Time altered
She sheds her skin for the wind and the rain

from coil
to river
from cradle
to grave

3

from birth to battle
with sharp tool and red ochre
vision-questing in the valley
others came here...
and left their mark

wind-faded, water worn
the mark lies waiting to be stolen by time

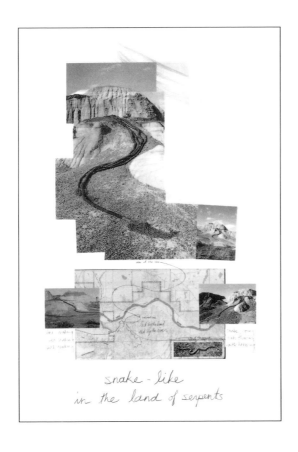

snake - like
in the land of serpents

circling - altar-ed
in the sacred place

4

line-making
river-snaking
earth-quaking

snake going
river flowing
earth-knowing

led by the land
red... by the river

5

red circle turned
in the place of the bloods

written on stone
where the Milk River floods

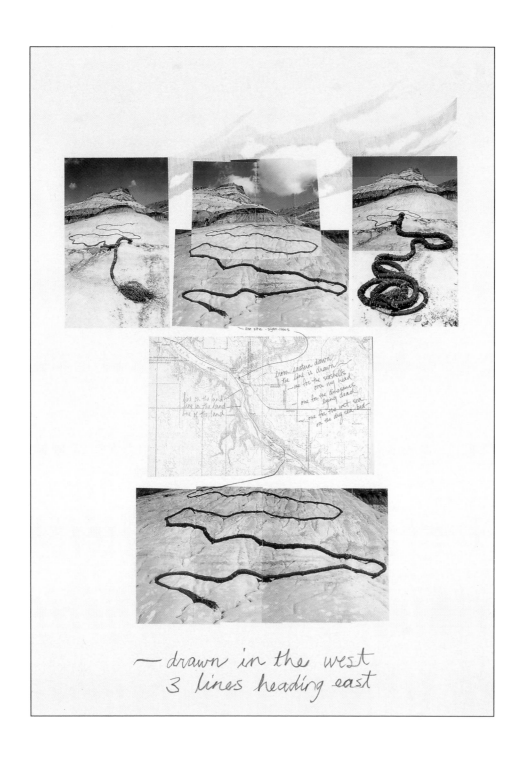

— drawn in the west
3 lines heading east

6

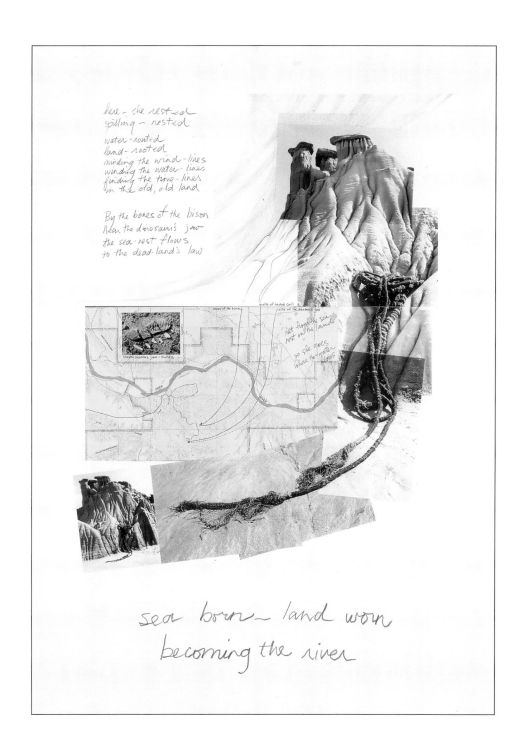

here – she rested
spilling – nested

water-rooted
land-rooted
minding the wind-lines
winding the water-lines
finding the time-lines
in the old, old land

By the bones of the bison
Near the dinosaur's jaw
the sea-nest flows
to the dead-land's law

sea born – land worn
becoming the river

7

List of Plates: *the Alberta Badlands Series*

The works represented here were selected from a
series of 9 Biographical Notes from the Alberta Badlands.

japan
1993

ordinary
in the Orient
common
on the wharf
ocean-tossed
culture-crossed
from origin
to source

The Coil *on site in Japan, 1993*
(from top to bottom)

at a Shinto shrine near Hita

in a public garden, Tokyo

on a fishing wharf, Ito-shima, Kyushu

at Futamigaura, Kyusshu

one rope tied
by Shinto hands

one laid down
from distant land

one for binding
one for finding

both bound by
the sea — the sand

one to lead
a caring eye
one to wed
2 rocks to tie

one to map —
reveal a site
one to manifest
a rite 法留

meoto-iwa
married rocks
shimenawa
sacred rope
umi - sea
ishi - stone
komichi - path
nazomi - rope

七五三縄

leading -- led
-- to the sacred rope

1

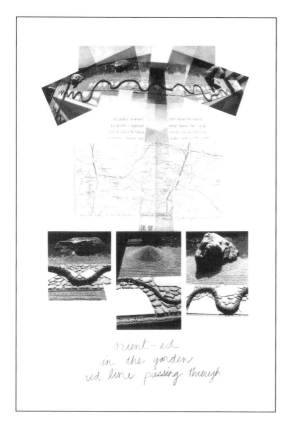

orient - ed
in the garden
red line passing through

en-circling — a sumo ring

2

occidental - oriental
accidental - planned
from the wild - to the tamed
to a path - stone and sand

sand marks the water
stone marks the lands
raked sand and red rope
make marks - of the hand

a line to lead, a line to heed,
through shadow, through light
to feed, to be freed

3

male wrapped by female
the circles are placed
by the cord of a woman
a man's rope, embraced

circling on a sumo ring
no woman's foot may tread
her line is laid without trespass
his circle, encircled - red

his sacred power ring,
her hand... empowering

*traps—trapped
a vicious circle*

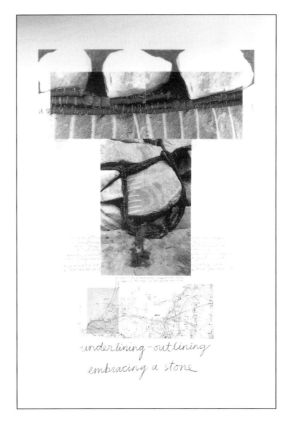

*underlining-outlining
embracing a stone*

4

*from sparse to dense
decline to rise
abundant……… scarce
the line still lies*

*old trap bound   new traps found
old hunter wrapped   new hunters trapped
a circle turned   a cycle spurned*

5

*one grey stone…immutable
seven lines…inscrutable
enduring, persistent
eternal they stand
a permanent mark, a transformable land*

*one red rope…ephemeral
a transient line…amenable
provisional, temporal
a fugitive sight
a fleeting mark, a transformative rite*

6

STILL LIFE (?) on the wharf
nesting with the nets
fish hunters
fish eaters
feeders
depleters?
bounty-hunters'
bounty-caught...
in sustenance lies
food for thought
法留
nets to entangle, tools to ensnare
one role to nourish, one to impair
to harvest, to feed, to ravage, to bleed
to consume and deplete or renew and repair
caught – bound
by the tools of the trade

7

List of Plates: *the Japanese Series*

The works represented here were selected from a
series of 12 Biographical Notes from Japan.

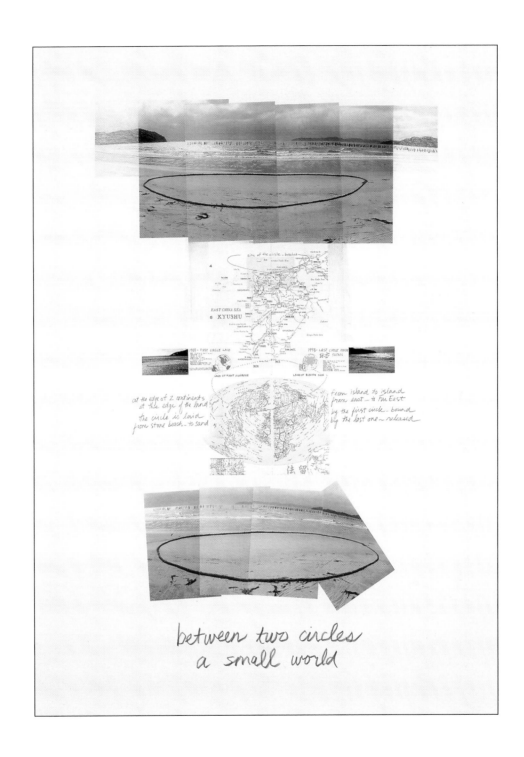

between two circles
a small world

8

Fragments from a Narrative

newfoundland...1988

Eli Tucker's wharf was one of the first places out of nature which pulled me ... Before it had always been remote places ...beach, barrens, the standing megaliths of northern islands. .. places distant from people. There was something strong there, at the wharf... smells that lured... objects and stuff that intrigued...echoes of a continuing ritual, a daily dance with the water. So I kept going back.

All the twine, the nets, the rope, the material tools of the trade, smelled of their function and history... webs, traps, lines... binding themselves and those who handled them, daily to the water-work, and yearly to the stories of each season. These lines to the water seemed to ground their handlers somehow... a tie between the land and the sea...summering in and out of the wet and wintering in the dry loft... I wanted something like that of my own, so with part of an old retired trap Eli gave me, I made the Coil... and with their help, began her life... water and land.

vancouver island...1990

On the way to Jordan River, Jim spots an eagle... points it out... it was a sweet start to a bitter day in the clear-cut slash... blackened ash, grey skies... red serpent in a ravaged garden... When I opened up the bag to remove the Coil and install her in the gallery in Victoria, there was an eagle feather lying unhurt beneath her bulk...

At East Sooke there was a big team... the landbag, the harnesses, a long trek with a long line ... I began to realize that perhaps the Coil was more about people than I had thought... that the gifts given by the crew extended far beyond their time and muscle... to include their eyes...

alberta badlands... 1991

There was a painter who helped Martin and I the first day in the East Coulee Badlands ... Marcel. He was, I think, pressed into service reluctantly, and was ambivalent about her until the first set-up was almost complete... loose line following land down a soft hill. He said, "..this is a drawing project !!!!... drawing..." My daughter Jordan once referred to her as "Mom's big, red line for drawing on the world with".

The second day at Writing on Stone, it was Jane and I alone...first time out on the land without men...no trouble with the 300 lbs. of Coil... the full day at one site, waiting for the light.

amherst island...1993

... hay field... all snow... bales scattered across white expanse. The "team" became concerned about footprints in the snow... They worked out a plan ... all time and labour, and wrapped a haystack leaving footprints only behind it... invisible to the camera.

japan...1993

Toru-san...Kuni's brother, Kuni... David's friend, David... Lesley's brother, Lesley... my friend.....following where the line may lead.

It was Toru-san who found us the West Coast Shima to stay in after we had done Futamiguara, who asked for permission to lay the Coil on the fishing wharves, who snoozed patiently in his car until the shooting was done, never complaining, never bored, always finding the way to wherever we needed to go.

In Tokyo and on the final day in Hita, at the shrine... Lesley and I alone... two women, and a heavy red rope, thousands of miles from home. She would stand and say, "wrap me" and length after length of the Coil would wind about her shoulders, like a heavy, red necklace. She would lead off, then... to where we would place it...me bringing up the rear with the remaining length of Coil... She could always carry more than I... a strong companion for the final journey.

St. John's, 1993

There were so many gifts from so many givers...

I remain deeply grateful for the help, assistance and support of the following individuals...all of them have made invaluable contributions to **The Coil's** brief but rich history on sea and on land. For their labour, their spirit, and their companionship along the way...I thank them...

for in the binding and the bending, lies the bonding....

1988-1989...In Newfoundland:

Eli Tucker, Caleb Tucker, Jamie Best, Paul Pope, Nigel Markham, Milton Spraklin Sr., and the staff of Norman Wade Co., St. John's, for their flexibility and good natured support throughout the project.

1990...On Vancouver Island:

Sue Donaldson, Jim Lindsay, Kelly Irving, Bob Preston, Kerry Francis, Roy Green, Paul Dishaw, Terryl Atkins, John Orser, Jill Ehlert

1991...In the Alberta Badlands:

David and Marie Kaufman, Ed Jurewicz and Grace Jefferies, Katy McKelvey and Steve Nunoda, Nigel Markham, Duane Nickerson, Yvonne Markotic and Martin McSween, Marcel Duschenes, Jane Evans, the Calgary Society of Independent Filmmakers,
and the staff of Dinosaur and Writing-on-Stone Provincial Parks.

1993... on Amherst Island, Lake Ontario:

Jan Winton, Adam Fingret, Andrew Butkevicius, Cheryl McCormick, Jennifer Essex, Ingrid Dabringer, Becky Soudant, Mandy Gerland, Leah Balfe,
John and Maribeth Hall,
Department of Art, Department of Film Studies,
and the Agnes Etherington Art Centre, Queen's University

1993... in Japan

Lesley Pechter, David Wynne, Miki Maruta, Tony Concil, Nobi Nagasawa,
Ross Reid, Kuni and Toru Kajiwara, Yakeo Okui, Kevin Feilder,
Pierre Deslormes of the Canadian Consulate in Fukuoka,
Beverly Mack and Claude Savard of External Affairs Canada,
Akiko Nawata, Louis Hamel, and David Anido of the Canadian Embassy in Tokyo

with special thanks to Victor Young of F.P.I., St. John's
and extraordinary thanks to Strat and Jordan Canning.

Pam Hall, 1993

Caleb, Pam, and Jamie on board the Whispering Sea... first day of sitework with the Coil on the water, North Atlantic, 1988

Jamie with the Coil at Middle Cove Beach, 1988

Jim and the Coil, reclining in the clearcut slash near Jordan River, Vancouver Island, 1990

Roy, Kerry, Bob, and Kelly, using the landbag harnesses for the first time, East Sooke, Vancouver Island, 1990

Duane, circling in the Badlands, Writing on Stone,
near Milk River, Alberta, 1991

Some of the Queen's crew, preparing to wrap a stack (top), and
the stack they wrapped (bottom), Amherst Island, Ontario, 1993

Lesley, wrapped with the Coil in a Tokyo garden, (right), and
with Toru-san unbagging the Coil on the fishing wharf at
Shima, Kyushu (above). Japan, 1993.

Pam Hall: Biography

Pam Hall was born in Kingston, Ontario, in 1951. She graduated with an Honours B.F.A. from Sir George Williams University, in Montreal in 1973, and from the University of Alberta in 1978 (M.Ed.). She has lived in St. John's, Newfoundland since 1973.

Principal Solo Exhbitions

1993
Tools of the Trade, Canadian Mission, New York, (for the United Nations Meetings on High Seas Fishing)

Inshore Artifacts, Meeting of Like-Minded Countries on High Seas Fisheries, St. John's, Newfoundland

The Coil that Binds... Agnes Etherington Art Centre, Queen's University, Kingston, Ontario

1992
The Coil that Binds...(the Newfoundland Work), Art Gallery of Nova Scotia, Halifax, N.S.

The Coil that Binds, the Line that Bends:The West Coast Work, Acadia University Art Gallery, Wolfville, Nova Scotia

1991
INSHORE ARTIFACTS, Christina Parker Fine Art, St. John's

Sidewinding in the Badlands:The Coil that Binds, the Line that Bends, The New Gallery, Calgary, Alberta

1990
The Coil that Binds,the Line that Bends,the Western Journey, Open Space,Victoria, B.C.

1989
The Coil that Binds,the Line that Bends, Sir Wilfred Grenfell Art Gallery, Cornerbrook, NFLD.

1988
Lunar Legends, Christina Parker Fine Art, St. John's, Newfoundland

Worshipping the Stone, Mount Saint Vincent University Art Gallery, Halifax, N.S.

In the Temple, Eastern Edge Gallery, St. John's

1987
Worshipping the Stone, Memorial University Art Gallery, St. John's, Newfoundland

Principal Group Exhibitions:

1991
NO FISHING, Resource Centre for The Arts, St. John's

Canada at Bologna, Academy House, Toronto, Ontario

1990
Canada at Bologna, an exhibition of Canadian children's book illustrations, Bologna, Italy

1989
MASKUNOW: a path,a trail,curated by Joan Borsa, Memorial University Art Gallery, St. John's

1988
Sound Symposium,outdoor installation entitled Path to the Wishing Place at St.Michael's, NFLD.

City and Sea, curated by Marlene Creates, MUN Art Gallery, St. John's, NFLD.

1987
Innovation:Subject and Technique, U. of T. Gallery, Scarborough Campus, Toronto

1986
25 Years of Newfoundland Art:Some Significant Artists, organized by MUN Gallery, St.John's, (toured to Beaverbrook Gallery, Fredericton, N.B., Cambridge Art Gallery, Cambridge Ontario)

NewFound Artists Land, MUN Gallery, St. John's, ARTSPACE, Peterborough, Ont., SAW Gallery, Ottawa, KAAI, Kingston, Ont.

Collections
City of St. John's
Hibernia Management Development Corporation
Royal Bank of Canada
Radisson Corporation
Fishery Products International
Toronto Dominion Bank
Bank of Montreal
Memorial University Permanent Collection
Government of Newfoundland and Labrador
Department of External Affairs,Canada
Canada Council Art Bank
Private Collections in Canada and Great Britain

List of Works in the Exhibition

Biographical Notes

...from the Newfoundland Series:

1 a bending, a binding... a berth on the water*
2 sea-water wet... coiled on the deck
3 drawn by the fish-killers to Eli's Wharf
4 a line, a life, a past, a dream...
5 his net, her nest, at rest*
6 first sign ~ first site... coiled line ~ in-sight*
7 lie lightly on the land
8 spell-binding on the barrens*
9 serpentine in the snakeless land*
10 red circle ~ stone circle... re-turning ...*
11 coiled from a fish-killer's trap...*
12 at rest on ancient calculi...

...from the Vancouver Island Series:

13 feng shui in the west*
14 dragon-guarded in the west... re-turning east*
15 safe-harboured... on the sea wall*
16 stone circle re-turned...*
17 uterine...she lies revealed*
18 concealed in the belly~ revealed on the land*
19 uprooted ~ in the sacred grove*
20 which the serpent ~ which the garden ?
21 stretched mark ~ stretch marks

...from the Alberta Badlands Series:

22 half-moon hoodoo... wrapped ~ enrapt
23 earth bound... on ancient ground*
24 drawn in the west...3 lines heading east*
25 circling ~ altar-ed...in the sacred place*
26 a transient line...writing on stone*
27 snake-like in the land of the serpents*
28 ...cradled in the grave*
29 sea born ~ land worn...becoming the river*

...from the Japanese Series:

30 path-finding... in the garden*
31 underlining ~ outlining... embracing a stone*
32 orient-ed... in the garden...*
33 caught ~ bound... by the tools of the trade*
34 traps ~ trapped... a vicious circle*
35 rope to rope ~ net to net...*
36 bound ~ inclined... to seek ~ to find*
37 a line ~ enshrined*
38 en-circling ~ a sumo ring*
39 recumbent in the Far(ther) East*
40 leading ~ led... to the sacred rope*
41 between two circles... a small world*

from excerpts from a long line being drawn on the land

42 fragments, site-dependent photo-installation*

NOTE: All *Biographical Notes* are mixed media on paper, and are 44" (height)x 30"(width) with the following exceptions;

13 diptych, 68" x 30", m.m. on paper with colour photograph
14 diptych, 64" x 30", m.m. on paper with colour photograph
15 diptych, 68" x 30 ", m.m. on paper with colour photograph
20 triptych, 44" x 84"
21 triptych, 30 " x 104"
22 four panels, 74" x 90", m.m. on paper with colour photographs
42 dimensions variable, 12-24 photo-panels, 11" x14" each

This List of Works refers to the exhibition at the Art Gallery of Memorial University of Newfoundland.
All works marked with * are included in the Tokyo exhibition. The Canadian touring exhibition includes all those marked with * but only 7 from *the Japanese Series.*